TABLE OF CONTENTS

Other Books by XENA

Paws of a Sculptor:
Things to Do with Clay Litter

•

The Moon, the Alley and You:
A Love Story

•

Chicken Soup for the
Kitty Bowl

DEDICATION

No book is ever written by a single cat. This is no exception. In my life I have had many mentors, even a human or two, who have helped me to stay on the path. My thanks to them and to all of you who now take up the challenge of "helping your human to be."

INTRODUCTION

To be honest I had a few reservations about writing this book because some cats do not think it would be to our advantage to share our knowledge with humans. Having carefully considered all sides of the argument, (that is, I slept on it) I have come to the conclusion that it's time we honor our humans by sharing our wisdom with them. In the sharing, the giving and the receiving, we will all eventually know "the way."

Over the years my mom has told me stories about some cats she calls "legends." She wanted me to include their tales in my book but I reminded her that pictures are worth a thousand words. This is especially true with us. On the last page of each chapter you will find some of these legends. Enjoy their presence on your journey, as I do.

Xena (pronounced 'Zena')

Frequently asked questions

Can humans really be understood?

How long does it usually take to get a human in shape?

How can we measure their success?

How do you figure a human's age in cat years?

For answers, read on.

CHAPTER ONE

Walking Your Talk

We live "in the moment," which is something that humans rarely do. Although we try to teach them by example, they continue to dwell on the past and worry about the future, and no amount of catnip seems to help.

As cats we never really need to be anywhere, since wherever we are, we are there because we choose to be, just as we are who we are because we choose to be. These are some of the things we can and should teach our humans. "Walking your talk" is the best teaching tool at your disposal. Even though it may appear to have no effect it is important to persevere for your human's sake, and yes even for your own.

We would survive quite well without humans, but there are some perks in having them around. For instance, the only real hunting I do these days is sniffing out where the treats are kept. Also, a warm lap sure beats the cold ground. Sharing your home with people can be a good experience if you take the time to teach them "the way."

Helping humans starts at home

When it comes to making a space work, cats are *Feng Shui'd* to the max. All spaces work for us, even those occupied by something or someone else. This can be achieved in every room in

The Way of the Cat

The Cat Box

Thousands of years ago, cats were worshipped as gods. Cats have never forgotten this.

—Anonymous

the house without moving the furniture. Right now let's look at some of the things you can do to, and for various rooms in the house.

The living room

The living room is the hub for human activity. It is where they read, entertain, rest, watch television, where they meditate (this involves sitting in the recliner chair with their eyes closed) and just kind of hang out. It is more central to humans than even the kitchen, which should tell you a little about their priorities. Following are a few exercises to help you get started on your journey to helping your humans:

1. Your mom is lying on the couch holding a book in front of her. In a few minutes, after she has gotten involved

in the story, jump up and lie on the book. If she scoots you off (highly unlikely) just jump back up as often as it takes for her to stop scooting and start stroking. Whether it takes a few jumps or she starts stroking you immediately, let her continue for a few minutes and soon she will begin to fall asleep. When you are sure your mom is asleep move up to her chest and stare at her, sort of vulture-like. Eventually this will help her learn a level of alertness even as she sleeps.

2. While your mom is sitting listening to the stereo, climb up into her lap and immediately go to sleep. In a short time she will start trying to move a little without disturbing you, to get the blood in her immobilized arms

---

The Cat Box

A kitten is chiefly remarkable for rushing about like mad at nothing whatsoever, and generally stopping before it gets there.

Agnes Repplier 1855-1950—Human.

The Way of the Cat

The Cat Box

The way she walks, the way she stalks, the way she "talks," makes even the most ordinary cat extraordinary.

Peter Collier 1849-1918—Human

and/or legs moving again. Let her wiggle a little longer then give a sharp little cry and then jump down giving her a dirty look as you slowly walk away. This lesson can go a long way to teaching your mom about stamina.

3. For some of you whose humans have a television the size of a wall, this next exercise is probably not feasible, but for the rest of you it can be entertaining and hopefully it will teach them how to see around any obstacles in life. When your humans are settled comfortably in front of the television, hop on top and let your tail swing slowly back and forth in front of the screen. Watch out for any little kitty toys that come flying your way. This exercise also works on computer monitors (see The Office).

4. With this next lesson you may get them to turn off the television and focus their attention completely on you. Fall asleep on the remote control. They will get up and change the station by hand (if they remember how to

do that) rather than disturb you. Since they are not used to having to watch more than five minutes of the same show they will probably turn it off and come over and pet you. Stay alert here though, they may be just trying to distract you to get you off the remote control.

5. Use the stereo speakers as a stretching and scratching post. If they didn't want us to do this they wouldn't call them "woofers." There aren't any real lessons for the humans in this one or the next, but sometimes it is important to take care of your own needs first.

6. Draperies—need I say more? Also keep in mind, as my friend Sprite pointed out, the cords from blinds can be quite fun, and it's possible to get the whole darn blind

The Cat Box

The trouble with humans is they can't seem to remember what it is they are supposed to be doing but they are still in a terrible hurry to get it done.

Zodiac

The Cat Box

Of all animals, he alone attains the Contemplative Life. He regards the wheel of existence from without, like the Buddha. There is no pretense of sympathy about the cat. He lives alone, aloft, sublime, in a wise passiveness.

Andrew Lang 1844-1912—Human

to fall down. Humans don't enjoy this kind of fun as much as we do, so it's best to run and hide when they become aware of your activities.

7. To teach people a sense of community, greet all guests as they arrive at the front door and if you hear one say "cat allergies" visit with him the entire evening. You might want to bring along some tissue with you as a friendly gesture.

8. Does your mom use a feather duster? Jump on it while she is dusting and slide across the table. This will save her valuable dusting time and teach her to accept help.

9. Crawl under furniture where only you can fit and then make sure your mom sees you when you come out covered with dust bunnies. This will work in any room in

the house and she will really appreciate you pointing out places that need to be cleaned.

The kitchen

Even though your humans probably won't feed you every time they go into the kitchen, it might be a good idea to follow them there and give them a hand with whatever it is they are doing. And you will be able to hear the can opener better.

1. Help your humans stay organized in the kitchen. If they are cooking, push things off the counter and turn over

---

Dear Xena,

The dust bunnies are getting so big in our house that they are starting to scare me. Some of them look big enough to hide another cat. How can I get my mom to clean them up?

Pugsley in Pawtucket

Dear Pugsley,

Wait for a time when your mom is going out someplace and she gets dressed in some nice dark blue or brown wool slacks; roll around in the biggest pile of dust bunnies you can find and without cleaning yourself—you can do it—jump up on her lap and snuggle in. I'm sure she'll see the problem and take care of it.

X

The Way of the Cat

The Cat Box

Watch a cat when it enters a room for the first time. It searches and smells about, it is not quiet for a moment, it trusts nothing until it has examined and made acquaintance with everything.

Jean Jacques Rousseau 1712-1778—Human

as many packages and containers as you can so that they focus on the main task.

2. Teach them the importance of being able to work with a handicap. If they are doing dishes, grab the sponge and run. They will try and finish with a dishrag and discover that it doesn't work nearly as well.

3. If they are just sitting at the table reading, try the "sit on the book" technique as in lesson one from the living room.

4. Keep as many toys as possible under the refrigerator just out of human sight and within your reach. These will more than likely be one of the dust bunny sites we discussed earlier and since they usually only get cleaned when you point out the problem, the toys should be safe. (Remember to remove all the toys before you do your dust bunny check.) When there are people milling around in the kitchen, bring out all of the toys and place them strategically near feet. This will help them learn to

walk through a mine field should the need ever arise. (Leave the kitchen in case someone trips over one.)

The laundry

1. Take a sock from the pile on the floor in the bedroom and squish it between the cushions on the couch. This is most effective when it is not discovered until there is company. When the moment is right, entertain the guests by pulling out the sock. Your human will learn a great deal about remaining cool in potentially embarrassing situations.

2. If your dad puts the freshly cleaned and dried clothing on the bed you have no choice but to snuggle up in it. When he returns to find the clean laundry covered with that "tell tail" grey, he'll learn to put things away.

The bedroom

The bedroom is my favorite room because you can really get into some one-on-one with your humans. It's the choice place for being right in their face.

The Way of the Cat

1. This, like the clean clothes lesson, will hopefully teach them to put things away. Humans can pile an amazing amount of stuff on the tops of their dressers. Oftentimes these things make great toys. A roll of postage stamps; a little plastic thing that makes the car beep before the human gets in (I guess they like to be greeted by their automobiles. Go figure.); a wadded up napkin with a phone number on it; earrings; cufflinks, and the list goes on. Once you have the toys you want picked out and safely hidden away, climb back up on the dresser and clear some space for a nap. After all, selecting toys can be tiring.

2. Your mom will require some help when changing the sheets on the bed. After she tucks one end of the sheet under the mattress she will go to the other end of the bed and pull the sheet up like a little sail before she tucks it in. Dive bomb head first under that sheet. Don't move a muscle. When she has tucked in the other end she won't

> **The Cat Box**
>
> *Time with humans is not always wasted.*
>
> Tony

> **The Cat Box**
>
> *Time with cats is never wasted.*
>
> Colette 1873-1954—
> Human

even notice that you are there. My mom rarely notices and when she does and pats me on the butt she experiences the "claws of life."

3. An easy way to teach your dad to close the closet door is to have an all day adventure in there while he is at work. These multi-leveled expanses are filled with many soft and snuggly things. Getting up to the higher levels is a breeze via the sleeve of a heavy wool jacket, and once on the upper level there are so many things that need rearranging. After that? A nap on that nice soft cashmere sweater. While you are on the lower level remember that shoes are an excellent place to hide toys.

4. Another way to help your mom in the bedroom is to jump into the bed after you have eaten your breakfast. By choosing to sleep there, you will provide the excuse she needs to leave the bed unmade.

The bathroom

1. Sit on the edge of the bathtub while your dad is taking a bath and stare at him. It will make him uncomfortable

The Cat Box

Everything that moves, serves to interest and amuse a cat. He is convinced that Nature is busying herself with his diversion; he can conceive of no other purpose in the universe.

François-Augustin Paradis de Moncrif
1687-1770—Human

and he won't stay in the water too long and get all wrinkly. Also, you will be furthering the cause for water conservation because he will probably take fewer baths.

2. Hide objects that you think may be a danger to them. My mom has this weird looking thing that she uses in the shower. It looks like a big mesh flower and I decided it wasn't good for her so I hid it. She just went and bought another one. Sometimes no matter how hard you try, you can't help humans. Oh, that reminds me, I should try and find the other one I hid, it could look like a dust *cow* by now.

3. To teach your humans to look before they leap, put a few toys in the bathtub or on the shower floor. If they turn the shower on without looking they will step on a soggy, furry mouse toy and I guarantee they'll never turn the water on again without looking. This is an impor-

tant lesson because you could be in there taking a nap when that awful, wet water flows.

4. Don't forget the toilet paper roll. I have a personal best of unrolling 750 sheets into a beautiful, sculptured pile on the floor.

5. Knock their toothbrushes on the floor when you notice that the bristles are worn and the brush needs replacing. Finally, remember the bathroom is a pretty small space so if you are there helping them brush their teeth, watch your tail and their feet.

The office

Many, many humans work at home these days mostly so they can be near their cats, and since the computer has helped to make this possible it is in your interest to understand the workings of the digital demon.

1. Something you will notice right away is that thing they call a mouse. This is not even a good imitation. If it were a living, breathing mouse, it would not just sit there when I walk into the room. You can bat it around a little bit if you want, but it isn't a mouse and you don't need to capture it for your

The Way of the Cat

human. Don't be discour-
aged though, there are
plenty of other ways you
can help in the office.

2. Generally, you will see
   your mom either giving
   the mouse a little squeeze
   or tapping away at the
   keyboard. Sometimes
   though she just sits and
   stares at the monitor.
   There are a number of
   things you can do to free her from the monitor's spell.
   Walking across the keyboard is one of them. It will get
   her attention very quickly if the screen suddenly turns
   blue. Another way to break the spell is the same as the
   television exercise. Jump up on the monitor and face
   the wall with your tail hanging in front of the screen. Or
   turn around and lie down on top of the monitor and
   try and catch that little arrow that moves around.

3. The computer isn't the only thing you can help with. If
   your dad keeps a bin filled with paper clips, push pins,
   pens and lots of other stuff and it is a real mess, you can
   push it off the shelf. That way when he picks everything up he can reorganize and maybe even clean the
   cookie crumbs out of the bin.

4. An office assistant would be of little value without tele-
   phone skills. Can you answer the phone when it rings?

The Cat Box

What greater gift than the love of a cat?

Charles Dickens 1812-1870—Human

Can you take it off the hook so that it doesn't ring and disturb your human? Can you erase the messages left on the answering machine by stepping on the flashing red light? Practice these procedures and your person will give you lots of attention.

The right place at the right time

Humans are creatures of habit, thus making our lives much easier. They can be counted on to create a fairly regular schedule and stick to it. This predictability will give you the opportunity to plan and live a comfortable, catered to, cared for life, thus keeping your human happy.

Use the hours they are out of the house to establish the ideal locations for perching, sleeping, hiding, dive bombing, practicing your "looks" in the mirror and all of the other things they think come naturally. Try out every chair or flat space you can find for sleeping, bathing, etc. and check out the proximity of the nearest exit should someone show up unexpectedly.

Here are some tips to determine the quality of a location.

1. Can you hear most, if not all of what is being said or done? Listen for the sound of a can opener, if you can hear it the location gets high marks.

2. Are you in a place where a human who can't see in the dark may kick or step on you? Subtract a number of points for this.

A rug is a challenge that must be met head on.

The Cat Box

*Cleanliness in the cat world is usually a
virtue put above Godliness.*

Carl Van Vechten 1880-1964—Human

3. Locations should be comfortable, although comfort is relative. My cousin Gracie likes to sleep on her mom's answering machine and press the buttons when the phone rings.

4. Give yourself high points for finding a spot that requires your dad to be inconvenienced. This will teach him generosity. This is not a new concept. Muezza, the cat who lived with the Prophet Mohammed, got Mohammed to cut a piece of cloth off his robe in order to go to prayer without waking him. As it should be.

5. A spot that your human has just cleaned can be rewarding and will help teach him the impermanence of all things.

6. Windowsills are a good choice. People going past the house will point and say things like "Oh look, a kitty, how cute." And your human will be more apt to notice that the windows need washing.

Keeping your human in shape

1. Can you produce a hairball on demand? If you can it is probably one of the best ways to get your dad up and moving. You don't really have to produce the actual

hairball, just the sounds and movements associated with that action should be enough. If you happen to be the first cat your dad has ever lived with, you may need to produce one or two actual hairballs to get him trained. After that you should have him flying off the sofa with the first little telltale sound.

2. People have a great amount of stamina when it comes to opening and closing doors for you. Just sit in front of a door and look like you want to go through it. Someone will see you and open the door. Of course, once

the door is open, you will turn around and walk away. This can be very good for their biceps if repeated often enough. Remember it is their health we are concerned about here.

3. Humans love to play with those little toys and balls they are always buying and shoving in your face. Humor them and at the same time you can help them get a little more exercise. I WILL NOT retrieve toys when my mom decides to play. She retrieves all of my toys and actually seems to enjoy it. Sometimes I suspect it takes her awhile to even notice that I have left the room. Just because I don't fetch when my

> **The Cat Box**
>
> *I am indebted to the species of the cat for a particular kind of honorable deceit, for a great control over myself, for characteristic aversion to brutal sounds, and for the need to keep silent for long periods of time.*
>
> Colette 1873-1954— Human

mom wants to play doesn't mean that I won't get involved in a spirited game of cellophane ball. The legendary Pete would bring the crumpled cellophane to his mom and drop it at her feet. If she didn't respond right away he would keep nudging it toward her until she finally decided to get involved. They would throw and catch and bat it around for awhile and then when Pete was tired of playing, he would carry the cellophane into the kitchen and drop it in his water bowl. Game over. A perfect technique for teaching people that they are not always in control.

4. Another good way to get them moving a little when you are playing with a toy is to bring it close to them, but not close enough for them to grab it. As they stretch to get the toy, back up, just a little at a time so they have to keep moving a little closer. I think they really like this game and the stretching is good for them.

5. Cardiovascular exercises can be very good for your human. One time I brought my mom a mouse at 3 a.m. The mouse wore his running shoes whereas my mom was barely awake. We chased and chased and chased, opened closets, closed closets, opened doors, closed doors. Finally when my mom had gotten the mouse real close to the front door, she flung it open and tried to chase the mouse the rest of the way out, but he had disappeared. The only thing that stood between where the mouse had last been seen and the front door was a small file cabinet on rollers. My mom stood with her feet spread, a broom in her right hand, the

top of the cabinet in her left and slowly she began to lean the cabinet over. That was when I decided to jump in and help. The mouse darted out, Mom tried to grab me and the file cabinet fell over on it's side. Yep, you got it. My mom had spent an hour trying to catch the mouse to keep me from killing it and she dropped a wooden file cabinet on it. It was not a pretty sight, but the result was worth it. My mom's heart was pumping like crazy.

Cats and cars

We don't often ride around in cars. When we do it is usually on the way to our physician's office and usually inside one of the small prison cells that humans seem to like so much. But there was a cat, Seth, (rest his gentle soul) who rode comfortably in the passenger's seat of his mom's convertible Mercedes…with the top down. Seth never did say how he convinced her to let him ride this way so unless one of you out there has some ideas, best we continue to submit to *The Cage*.

I do like to lie on the top of my mom's car in the evening to watch the sunset. I don't go up there during the day because in this New Mexico sun I would be a cooked cat in no time at all. Sitting up on the roof gives me a better view of what is going on. I have tried all the other cars around the neighborhood, but my mom's seems to work best. Besides, hers is the only one I can sit on without her yelling at me. Hers has the right amount of slant to the front and rear windows, the top is a perfect height for viewing and best of all is that it is located nice and close to my food source.

Although cars aren't a big part of our lives, they are a big part of humans' lives. Personally, I think they could do with a little more walking, running and mousing.

Remember, when we are "walking our talk" we do it with two legs on one side and then two legs on the other side. Besides us, only camels and giraffes walk with such style. All the other lower forms alternate left front, right back, right front, left back.

Legendary Cats
FROM XENA'S PICTURE GALLERY

Julio

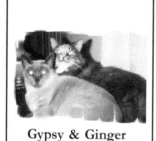

Gypsy & Ginger

Gracie

Benny

The Way of the Cat

CHAPTER TWO
When Do We Eat?

Eating comes second only to sleeping, although I doubt if even I could eat 12 to 16 hours a day. Suffice it to say, I like my food.

Humans have always wondered what we eat. Even poor Alice falling down the rabbit hole wondered:

Down, down, down. There was nothing else to do, so Alice soon began talking again. 'Dinah'll miss me very much to-night, I should think!' (Dinah was the cat.) 'I hope they'll remember her saucer of milk at tea-time. Dinah my dear! I wish you were down here with me! There are no mice in the air, I'm afraid, but you might catch a bat, and that's very like a mouse, you know. But do cats eat bats, I wonder?' And here Alice began to get rather sleepy, and went on saying to herself, in a dreamy sort of way, 'Do cats eat bats? Do cats eat bats?' and sometimes, 'Do bats eat cats?' for, you see, as she couldn't answer either question, it didn't much matter which way she put it. She felt that she was dozing off, and had just begun to dream that she was walking hand in hand with Dinah, and saying to her very earnestly, 'Now, Dinah, tell me the truth: did you ever eat a bat?' when suddenly, thump! thump! down she came upon a heap of sticks and dry leaves, and the fall was over. —Lewis Carroll

Have you ever wondered why people think we like fish? It's not as if they find many of us swimming in the rivers or creeks looking for dinner. How many cats have you seen hunt cows? People usually see us hunting mice or birds, or out here in New Mexico, lizards. I have yet to see a can of mouse- or lizard-flavored food in the cupboard. There is tuna, salmon, mackerel (what *is* mackerel?) and usually chicken and turkey. The chicken and turkey make some sense, but I think the whole fish thing started long ago when villag-

ers would entice us with fish heads to get us to hang around and keep rodents out of their stored foods. We came, we ate, we stayed.

Keep them guessing

How many open cans of cat food does your human keep in the refrigerator because you turned up your nose at the so-called food in them? The record is held by a Canadian kitty named Georgia whose humans had 18 different cans of opened, uneaten cat food on their refrigerator

Dear Xena,
My human is a terrible cook and he keeps trying to feed me things he has cooked for himself. It isn't just that I don't want to eat the stuff, but I don't think he should be eating it either. What should I do?

Wanda from Washington

Dear Worried;
Take the food your dad gives you and when he is not looking, find a place to hide it, preferably outside, because eventually he may find it in the house. As far as keeping him from eating it, that may be more difficult. Humans seem to have a gullet rather than a palate so they don't really taste the food anyway. Just try not to watch.

X

The Cat Box

The playful kitten with its pretty little tigerish gambols, is infinitely more amusing than half the people one is obliged to live with in the world.

Lady Sydney Morgan 1783-1859—Human

shelves. Georgia tells us they threw them all away after about a week and started the process all over again.

In training your humans to feed you, the important thing to remember is: Confuse them. This will keep their brains active and stave off the cerebral sluggishness that comes in their later years.

- If they serve you tuna on Tuesday, take one little nibble and sulk. When they put down a different dish of food in hopes of stopping your sulking, go gaga over it. Then the next time they serve you tuna, and they will, go gaga over *it*, keeping in mind that whatever they serve after the tuna you simply look at with disdain. The main thing is to let them think they've figured out what you like to eat. If your human does not stick around to see if you

According to The Guinness Book of Records, *Himmy, an Australian tabby, weighed over 46 pounds.*

The Way of the Cat

like the food, do what my friend, Pete, did. If he didn't like what was served he would drag the throw rug over and cover the food dish with it. Pete definitely knew how to make a statement that could not be misinterpreted.

- If you hear your dad opening a can, climb out of whatever safe little cubby hole you were tucked into and dash into the kitchen. Start rubbing his leg or jumping up on the counter. If possible, rub against the hand that holds the can opener; this will help him open it faster. If he is opening something for himself he will be unable to eat it with you sitting there staring at him. He will try and bribe you with a treat. Ignore it and continue to stare at whatever he is having. When he finally caves under the pressure and gives you a small piece of his food, sniff it, shake your head sadly, give him that "You eat this garbage?" look and walk away.

I have been playing a little game with my mom. I have never eaten anything that came in a can. Never. But whenever she is opening one I come tearing across the house and jump up on the cabinet and try to smell the contents. She gets a puzzled look on her face, but none the less after she has opened it she puts it under my nose to

smell. I take a good long sniff and then turn around and walk away. She may think I'm just trying to make sure the food is safe for her to eat.

- Rarely are humans up at 4 a.m. In fact it may be necessary to wake them if they haven't gotten up by 6 to feed you. Try jumping into bed and sitting on their stomach or kneading their bladder. They have been in bed all night and may need to get to the litter box in a hurry if you gently remind them. This will also help them spend less time sleeping and more time kittying.
- If they are a little slow in the morning they may get to the kitchen and forget to feed you. A cat NEVER begs to be fed but there are many ways to remind them that nothing is more important than feeding you. Jump up on the table; jump up on their lap; scratch on a cabinet

door; stay within three inches of their feet so they trip over you (this takes a little practice to avoid serious injury); or get into their face and stare. You know the look. Marvin, in Bemidji, Min-

The Way of the Cat

nesota simply sits in the middle of the floor, close to his bowl. This gives his dad a choice: trip over him or fill the bowl. Unlike myself, Marvin also has an outside bowl. To make sure that that one gets filled, when his  dad opens the door to let him out, Marvin stands in the doorway holding the door open until his dad figures it out. You see, eventually they do get it.

• We are carnivores, but there is nothing like a little tall grass to nibble on now and then. My mom grows trays of what she calls "wheat grass" and remarkably she cuts off chunks and chews on them herself. I'm not totally sure what the health risks are to me by sharing, but I guess you have to take a chance every now and then.

The Cat Box

I believe cats to be spirits come to earth. A cat, I am sure, could walk on a cloud without coming through.

Jules Verne 1828-1905—Human

The Cat Box

The clever cat eats cheese and breathes down rat holes with baited breath.

W. C. Fields 1880-1946—Human

- Treat time can be a wonderful opportunity for personal growth—your human's, not yours, of course. The people who make all the kitty foods and treats wrap them in packages that appeal to your human, and often this has little to do with the quality of the food or whether you will like it.

Have you ever wondered where they get those cats they put on the packages? Their faces say, "I am a cat that never scratches people or furniture. A cat that eats whatever food you buy for me. I never have hairballs, or mess outside of the litter box. My fur is soft and clean and I do not shed. I love this food—buy

The Way of the Cat

it for your cat today, and she could be just like me." I can see these cats in their rug-lined dressing rooms sharing bottled water and imported salmon, laughing hysterically after the photo shoot. They are at the pinnacle of their careers, having climbed the precarious ladder from family photo album, to calendar cat to cat food package. Their fame may be fleeting but all the scratching and clawing has been worth it and that's why they look so happy on those cans and bags. I've also heard that many of those photos have been retouched.

- Although catnip is an herb and not really a food, it is a joy to sniff, snack and roll around in. Now I know that not all of you can enjoy catnip, it is some kind of genetic thing, but many of our distant cousins, the big cats, get a kick out of catnip too. Catnip is absolutely not addictive, so there is no chance of ending up in "The Kitty Ford Clinic." I like the fresh catnip my mom gets at the health food store. She tried to give me some  of the cheap, powdery stuff but I just turned up my nose and walked away. At one point she tried growing it but this was a disaster. I didn't have the heart to tell her that putting a catnip plant outside without protection was probably not a good idea in our neighborhood. I personally didn't touch it; it must have been Julio or Bennie or Sam or...

- Drink from your mom's cereal bowl when she is getting her coffee; she shouldn't be eating that much dairy. Remember, milk should be splashed at least as far as three inches from the bowl.

- When served that really juicy gourmet cat food, lick off the gravy and let the rest of the food dry up to look like beef jerky.

- Just so you know, you have to catch about five mice to equal the average meal your human serves you.

- It is very important to drink a lot of water and in order to do this as efficiently as possible you need to get your person to put water containers all around the house. The

The Way of the Cat

way I did it with my mom was to watch where she sat with a full glass of water. Then I would jump up and drink from her glass. I only needed to do this a couple of times for each location and she put out a glass for each of us.

- By "fast foods" humans do not mean mice or birds. They are talking about foods that come from "fast food" restaurants. These are generally hamburgers, French fries, chicken or other greasy items, wrapped in paper and crammed into a bag. If you see your humans come home with something like this— DON'T EAT IT! —and try dragging the bag out to the trash before your humans try to eat it. If you can't get rid of the bag of food at least hang around looking at your people in disgust while they eat it. Maybe they will think twice about bringing home the next greasy bag of "food."

The Cat Box

In a cat's eye, all things belong to cats.

—English Proverb

What humans tell other humans about feeding cats

I have been doing a lot of research in this area. (I go on-line a lot when

Mom is not home.) What I have found is that they have absolutely no idea what they are doing or saying. The following is a partial list of information I gathered from various human web sites on how to feed cats:

- Feed your cat twice a day.
- Feed your cat three times a day.
- Leave food out and let your cat eat whenever she wants.
- Do not leave food out for your cat all the time.
- Feed your cat dry food.
- Feed your cat canned food.
- Don't feed your cat table scraps.
- It is perfectly alright to feed your cat table scraps.
- Don't feed your cat treats.
- Your cats can have 10 to 15 percent of their daily allowance of food as treats.
- If your cat is fat put her on a diet.
- Do not put your cat on a diet.
- Do not make your own cat food.
- It is better for your cat if you make her food.
- Mix egg in your cat's food.
- Do not feed your cat eggs.
- Your cat can have one or two eggs a week.
- Don't try and force your cat to eat certain foods.
- You should determine your cat's diet. (HUH!)
- Give your cat vitamin supplements.
- Your cat doesn't need vitamin supplements.

And on, and on and on...

Well, you can see how confusing it is for your human to figure out what is best for you. Of course, that does not mean you have to make his job any easier by not being finicky. Finickyness is part of our charm and part of what makes our humans love us so much. My advice is that you show him what he is going to feed you as soon as it is catly possible. It will make his life much easier.

And remember, you are not trying to teach your human to be finicky, you are teaching him a greater appreciation for our finickyness. Just one more lesson on his journey to "be."

Bon Appétite!

Legendary Cats

Jack

Seth

Violet

Tippi

The Way of the Cat

CHAPTER THREE
Let a Sleeping Cat Lie

It is, of course, appropriate to dedicate an entire chapter to sleeping since we spend two-thirds of our lives doing it. This makes us experts on the subject and we are, therefore, beholden to pass this expertise on to the less-talented humans among us.

In the previous chapter I avowed that I loved eating second only to sleeping and boy, do I love sleeping. A typical day with my mom:

6:00-7:00 am	My mom gets up grumbling, puts on coffee, does her exercises, checks her emails and gets cleaned up to start her day.
6:00-7:00 am	I eat and then I sleep.
7:00-11:00 am	My mom starts working on her computer. She takes a break to eat some breakfast, and then she is back at work again.
7:00-11:00 am	I see if I can help my mom for awhile and then I sleep.
11:00 am-1:00 pm	My mom has lunch, reads a bit, answers her emails, gives me some treats and goes to get the mail.
11:00 am-1:00 pm	I eat my lunch, go outside for a leisurely walk, visit the litter box space of my choice, come in and have some treats and watch my mom for a few minutes.
1:00-5:00 pm	My mom is back to work.
1:00-5:00 pm	I sleep.
5:00-10:00 pm	My mom has dinner, checks all my water bowls, makes a few phone calls, reads for awhile and gives me a treat.
5:00-10:00 pm	I sleep and get up for a treat.

The Way of the Cat

10:00–11:00 pm	My mom gets ready for bed, closes the house up, reads for awhile.
10:00–11:00 pm	I sleep.
11:00 pm–6:00 am	My mom sleeps.
11:00 pm–6:00 am	I go out and hang out with some friends, wander around the neighborhood, go home and wake up my mom to tell her I'm home, sleep for a couple of hours, go out and sit on the porch for a couple of hours, go back in and wake up Mom to tell her I'm home, sleep for a couple of hours and eat.

Of course there can be variations in the day, but that is our preferred schedule. I think it works pretty well for both of us.

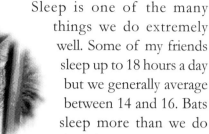

Sleep is one of the many things we do extremely well. Some of my friends sleep up to 18 hours a day but we generally average between 14 and 16. Bats sleep more than we do and so do opossums. They both check in at a grueling 20 hours a day. (If a cat catnaps and a bat batnaps, what do opossums do?)

People are not like us when they are sleeping. We can go from a deep sleep to being totally alert in a split second, while people tend to be groggy for quite awhile after they wake up. My mom has to drink her coffee in the morning before she can say anything more than "rrrrmmmmmpppphhhhhd sdfdsaj iead."

The Cat Box

Cats are rather delicate creatures and they are subject to a good many different ailments, but I have never heard of one who suffered from insomnia.

Joseph Wood Krutch 1893-1970—Human

The Cat Box

He seems the incarnation of everything soft and silky and velvety, without a sharp edge in his composition, a dreamer whose philosophy is sleep and let sleep.

Saki 1870-1916—Human

Our cousins in the wild had to be alert even when they slept. We still have many of the traits of our ancestors and can be ready to roll at the first sound of a can opener or treat bag. We can go back to sleep immediately if the sound turns out to be a false alarm.

Humans wonder why we sleep the number of hours we do. It is apparent that they have no idea how much energy it takes to keep things running smoothly around the house. The sleep helps us re-energize so that we can continue doing all the things we do so well.

The ultimate nap nook

Although anywhere is a nap nook for a cat, the ultimate nooks take a little research and development. Find it, fluff it and fold yourself neatly into or on it.

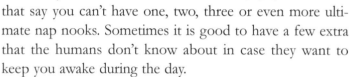

You need to discover your own nap nook and make it work for you. There are no rules that say you can't have one, two, three or even more ultimate nap nooks. Sometimes it is good to have a few extra that the humans don't know about in case they want to keep you awake during the day.

Since we are nocturnal beings we sleep more during the day. You know this and your dad knows this and still he tries to change you. Running around during the day, throwing toys, waking you out of a sound sleep—a not very subtle tactic to coax you into sleeping all night. Can you tell the wind when to blow?

The Cat Box

The cat pretends to sleep that it may see things more clearly.

Chateaubriand 1768-1848—Human

The Way of the Cat

The Cat Box

Of all God's creatures there is only one that cannot be made the slave of the leash. That one is the cat. If man could be crossed with a cat it would improve man, but it would deteriorate the cat.

Mark Twain 1835-1910—Human

Dear Xena,
My humans are always on the go and I want to do all I can to make life a little more peaceful around here. What can I do?

Jack in Chicago

Dear Jack;
We have talked about the ways that our mere sleeping can have a positive effect on your humans, but if it is really chaotic at your house you may have to pull out all the stops. Jump in their laps to sleep whenever possible, stay close to them at all times and purr, purr, purr.

X

Personally, I think the reason people want us to stay awake during the day is because they have the misguided notion that if we sleep at night, we will choose to sleep with them. A recent cat survey showed that 70 percent of humans want us to sleep on their bed whereas only 20 percent of us want to sleep with our humans.

One of my favorite places to sleep is in the laundry basket in the closet. I have my mom trained not to go digging around in the closet when I am "cat napping" and she has even put a small blanket on the bottom so I am more com-

fortable if there is no laundry in there. As I said, she is pretty well trained.

I try to change my "favorite spot" every six weeks or so to keep Mom guessing so that she doesn't go slamming doors and poking around

looking for me while I'm trying to sleep. If I want to be
available I sleep up on top of
a bookcase, which my mom
has thoughtfully covered
with a nice towel. She has so
much junk on her desk,
which is my flight path, that
she has to keep the printer

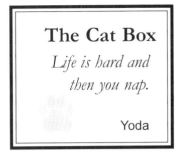

The Cat Box

*Life is hard and
then you nap.*

Yoda

closed up when she is not using it in order for me to climb
to the top. I hope she realizes that keeping the printer closed
keeps it clean and running more efficiently.

I am also not big on sleeping for many hours uninter-
rupted. I like to move around. Down from the bookcase,
into the closet, to the cabinet in front of the window, to

*Of all the toys your mom may try to get you to
play with, she is by far the best. With squishy
parts to knead on,
tangled hair to bat
about and a tummy
that will even
squeak when you
jump on it.*

the rocker and whenever my mom gets out of it—to the office chair for a nap. That does not usually turn out to be very long.

So, how, you ask me, does all this sleeping help our humans? Well, think about it. Their lives are pretty stressful and just having us around can be a calming experience. They always smile when they see us curled up in some unbelievably cute position and we know how good smiling is for people. Also, should they be paying attention, they would realize from our example just how many places there are to

The Cat Box

Cats sleep anywhere,
any table, any chair.
Top of piano, window-ledge,
in the middle, on the edge.
Open drawer, empty shoe,
anybody's lap will do.
Fitted in a cardboard box,
in the cupboard with your frocks.
Anywhere! They don't care!
Cats sleep anywhere.

Eleanor Farjeon 1881-1965—Human

The Way of the Cat

sleep. Outdoors in a nest of leaves, or on the grass under a shade tree in summer. Indoors they have couches, chairs, and even the floor which is good for their backs which they are always complaining about. Ah variety—truly the spice of life (and sleeping).

Well my friends, I could use a nap right now, so until the next chapter:

To sleep, perchance to dream...

Legendary Cats

Pugsley

Dolly

Sprite

Yoda

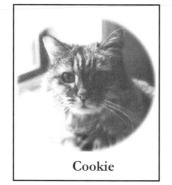

Cookie

The Way of the Cat

CHAPTER FOUR
*Our Furry Bodies,
Our Selves*

It never hurts to
know who you are and
how your various parts work. You may even be able
to impart a little of that knowledge to your human. Here
are just a few of the basics.

A cat by design

We are carnivorous mammals of the *Felidae* family and are well designed for hunting (and sleeping). We have somewhere around 60 thousand hairs per square inch on our backs and an amazing 120 thousand hairs per square inch on our cute little bellies. (I don't shed. I simply add to the texture and decor of our home.)

We have both an undercoat and an outercoat and we also have many more varieties of fur patterns and colors than our big cat brothers and sisters, because we no longer need to camouflage ourselves. But other than that we are pretty much the same cats we were thirty million years ago. With our sleek bodies, superb sight, excellent ears and remarkable leaping abilities we are hunting machines. To paraphrase a famous human philosopher: "I hunt, therefore I am."

The Cat Box

To please himself only, the cat purrs.

—Irish Proverb

The Way of the Cat

The Cat Box

A cat's eyes are windows enabling us to see into another world.

—Irish Proverb

We have over 230 bones and over 500 skeletal muscles. We don't have collar bones, the better to allow us entrance to anywhere we darn well please. Our spines are the reason for the suppleness of our movement. We have 30 vertebrae as opposed to 25 in humans and they have inflexible backbones and NO TAIL! We can run over 30 miles an hour and we can jump five to eight times our height, whereas

humans can jump only a little more than half their height. Hey Michael Jordan, how about a little one on one?

Our brains are more like human's than dog brains are. The order in rank *I* believe is cat brain, human brain and then dog brain.

It is even true that our brains contain an area that controls emotion just like the human brain. But really, when was the last time you sat and cried over a movie or a card you got in the mail? Let's just say we both have emotions—one species controls them and the other doesn't.

Because you are purr-fect

Humans don't seem to know why we purr. Why do cats do anything? Because we like to. How do we purr? We breathe air over our vocal cords causing vibrations and these vibrations are heard and felt throughout our bodies. A human theory says that purring is produced by rapid contractions of the muscles of the larynx. Good try folks, but I guess I oughta know. Humans generally think we purr when we are happy. Heck, we purr all the time—they just aren't paying attention.

As we see it

Our eyes are relatively larger than any other animal's and most of us do not have eyelashes. (A big savings in the mascara department.) We have an extra eyelid that is usually only visible if we don't feel well. We have great day and night vision, and excellent depth perception so we can hunt  and stalk from a distance, and then without warning, capture our prey. This also applies to those balls and toys your

The Way of the Cat

Dear Xena,

My humans give me a bath a couple of times a year. I don't go out and I'm a cat, for heaven's sake, I can bathe myself. Also I'm concerned that the shampoos will ruin the natural oils in my fur. What can I do?

Millie from Monee

Dear Millie;

You are right about the shampoo. I'm sure your humans think they are doing what is best, but of course they are mistaken. Do you still have your claws?

X

humans scatter around the house. Because of our large pupils we have much better night vision than our humans—quite an advantage when playing "catch me if you can." I know my mom has terrible night vision. Time and time again I've watched her stumble around the house at night and whenever she steps on one of my toys, she apologizes to it.

There is something you have to keep in mind when you are out and about in the evening hours. One of the reasons our night vision is so good is because of a special tissue behind the retina that reflects the light back out through our eyes causing them to literally "glow." This also makes

The Cat Box

The smallest feline is a masterpiece.

Leonardo Da Vinci
1452-1519—Human

us easy to spot, with the potential for turning *us* into prey.

One rather interesting, dare I say, "flaw" in our otherwise incredible vision is that we can't see something directly in front of our nose. We can smell it alright, we just don't see it and often will walk away from a few extra kibbles because we didn't see them.

We don't see colors the way most humans do. Unfortunately they don't know that and will buy toys that are bright red thinking they will be more interesting for us, when in fact what we see is a rather dull grey. But don't disappoint them. Pretend you like the red ball too.

We are all ears and then some

We have great hearing (the better to hunt with my dear) to compensate for a pretty questionable sense of smell. We hear much higher pitched sounds than our humans or their canine friends (our range is between 100 and 65

The Way of the Cat

thousand Hz), but the best thing about our ears is that they turn. Humans have six muscles for the outer ear, we have 30, giving us a sort of natural surround sound. We can rotate our ears 180 degrees and tune in on sound ten times faster than a dog.

Because of the way our ears are shaped, we can gather in sound and focus it into the ear channel. Since our hearing is three to four times more sensitive than our human's it is almost painful to listen to their TV or stereo. Feel free to use the remote to lower the volume on those noise boxes. If you do it in small increments your dad may not even notice and you will be doing him a great service by lessening the damage to his hearing too. Humans may yet learn that silence really is golden.

We also communicate a lot with the positioning of our ears. When we are quite comfy our ears are erect. On the rare occasion when we get scared, our ears are pressed back on our heads. When we are investigating something they are erect and pointing to the front. When we turn our ears backwards—watch out. I think my mom has finally nailed that one.

The Cat Box

If a cat does something, we call it instinct; if we do the same thing, for the same reason, we call it intelligence.

Will Cuppy
1884-1949—Human

Okay, I'll bite

We have 30 teeth: 12 incisors, 10 premolars, 4 felines, (oops) canines and 4 molars. Our canines grab on to our prey and because these teeth are embedded in sensitive tissue we can feel the prey's movement. Our incisors hold on to it, our molars and premolars chew it. I personally have totally massacred a number of little cloth mice with these ivories.

What do we use our tongues for?

I guess the question could more aptly be, "What *don't* we use our tongues for?" With the backward, scoop-like hairs that cover our tongues, we drink, eat and remain very well-groomed. Our tongues also have a special coating that removes old hair and dander. In addition it helps our fur stay waterproof.

Smells as sweet

As I said earlier, our sense of smell is not our strong suit, but we do have over 60 million olfactory cells and something called the Jacobson's Organ in the roof our mouth, behind our front teeth, that lets us analyze the air around us. (Some bats and reptiles have this organ too.) People think we are grimacing or making a face when we lift our lips to draw air over the organ, but we are just checking things out. I don't need any extra organ to smell catnip though, do you?

Making scents of things

We use almost our entire bodies to figure out what is going on, or has gone on around us. Humans often think that when we rub up against them we are showing them love or affection. In fact, we are actually protecting them from intruders by leaving our scent on them.

We have glands in our paws that leave our scent as we walk. Humans, of course, cannot smell this, but it is a great way to make our presence known to each other. We also have hairs like whiskers above our eyes and on either side of our mouths that take in information about our surroundings.

Our whiskers are special. They are stiffer than our fur and extremely sensitive. They are largely responsible for keeping us from banging into things when it is *totally* dark. Most of us have four rows of whiskers on our faces that we can push out for "feeling" our way around, or pull back flat in order to smell.

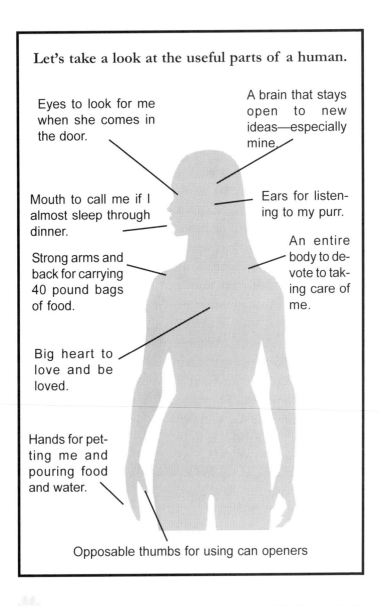

Let's take a look at the useful parts of a human.

Eyes to look for me when she comes in the door.

A brain that stays open to new ideas—especially mine.

Mouth to call me if I almost sleep through dinner.

Ears for listening to my purr.

Strong arms and back for carrying 40 pound bags of food.

An entire body to devote to taking care of me.

Big heart to love and be loved.

Hands for petting me and pouring food and water.

Opposable thumbs for using can openers

The Way of the Cat

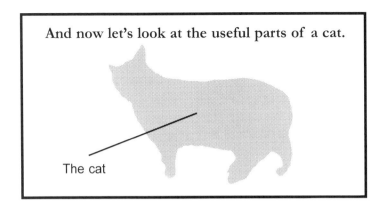

And now let's look at the useful parts of a cat.

The cat

All of our senses are fine-tuned and help us survive and keep our humans as safe as we possibly can. So sniff, sense, touch, listen, watch and most of all feel the vibrations in the air. Use your body with the precision it was designed for.

A tale of a tail

Ten percent of our bones are in our tail and because of that our tails help us stay balanced. I don't know about that. I kinda think that balance is every cat's middle name.

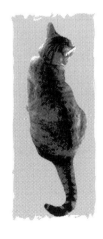

There has been quite a bit of human research on our tails and frankly it has taken a lot of the fun out of it. Many humans now think they can analyze our mood by the movement of our tail so it may be time to change our language a bit.

I mean it is one thing to help your humans but an entirely different thing for them to know (or think they know) what we are thinking. So, watch your back (side)!

Paws and jaws

We usually have five toes on our front paws and four toes on the back. Some of us though have extra toes on our feet, a condition known as polydactylism. We are the only species to walk on our claws instead of the pads of our feet.

Our jaws are pretty short but really strong. When we chomp down on our toys we can crush the catnip out of them. We can't move our jaws sideways so we get the most out of moving them up and down.

Grooming

No matter what you are doing, no matter what your human is doing, take a break and groom.

You have just knocked your mom's favorite coffee cup (filled with coffee) off the desk. While she is scrambling to wipe it up you can be cleaning and conditioning your fur.

The Cat Box

If I called her she would pretend not to hear, but would come a few moments later when it could appear that she had thought of doing so first.

Arthur Weigall 1880-1934—Human

Your dad has just come home from work and is frantic trying to get everything ready for some company this evening. Remind him that he hasn't fed you dinner yet and do the starving, ignored cat bit. As soon as he gets your food and puts it down in front of you, take a break and groom.

Of course, your grooming is not done to irritate your human. Quite the opposite. People have got to learn to relax, for the sake of all of us, and if they can see how you just stop, amidst noise and chaos, to take a relaxing grooming break, maybe they will get the idea. Of course grooming for them is a little more com-

plicated and involves getting under a stream of hot water (yuck!) but our lesson for them is not grooming, it's relaxing.

We groom not only to look our best, but also because we don't have sweat glands and it is necessary to apply the moisture that will evaporate and cool us off.

We do not need humans to groom us, besides they don't really seem to enjoy giving us baths any more than we enjoy getting them. Even so, they seem to think they can help us get clean. I was surfing the internet not long ago to see what was new in the way of cat stuff and I found a product that turned out to be premoistened, perfumed sheets that popped out so a human could wipe off his cat. Pulllleeeeeezzzz! It's the same product they sold humans to use on their babies bottoms. I don't think so. Anyway, you are in charge, so take care of your fur and everything that lies beneath it.

Do we age differently than humans? (notice I did not say grow up)

We age at a different rate than our human companions and because of that they may seem childish and immature.

Of course that is partially true, but what is also true is they have a lot more time to get as wise as us and still many of them never manage to. Here is a little chart that will show you how the aging in cats differs from humans in a form that humans like to call time.

Our years	Human years
6 months	10 years
8 months	13 years
1 year	15 years
5 years	36 years
10 years	56 years
15 years	76 years
20 years	96 years

Aging is as natural as sleeping. It is part of the great cycle we know as life. The secret is never to worry about how old you are but to know how well you lived every minute of every day. Cat's Truth.

So, aren't we remarkable creatures? Actually most humans find us not only physically remarkable but mysterious and intriguing as well. To us there's no mystery, it is our way of being.

Legendary Cats

Alex

Emily

Louise

Abby

The Way of the Cat

CHAPTER FIVE

Mumbles & Meows

COMMUNICATING WITH YOUR HUMAN

It may be as impor-
tant for us to speak to
humans as it is to speak
to each other. Both cats
and humans speak using
verbal   and   visual
"words." Unfortunately, both these words and the body
movements are communicated in different languages. One

The Cat Box

*My cat does not talk as respectfully to me as
I do to her.*

Colette 1873-1954—Human

of our greatest challenges in helping our humans is getting
them to understand what we are saying. Communication is
the key and speaking two entirely different languages doesn't
make that key turn smoothly.

Lewis Carroll wrote In *Alice Through the Looking Glass*,
"It is a very inconvenient habit of kittens that whatever

you say to them, they always purr. If they would
only purr for 'yes' and
mew for 'no', or any rule
of that sort, so that one
could keep up a conversation! But how can one
deal with a person if they
always say the same
thing?"

Well excuse me Mr.
Lewis, but just because
you don't understand

The Cat Box

It is difficult to obtain the friendship of a cat. It is a philosophic animal, strange, holding to its habits, friend of order and cleanliness and one that does not place its affections thoughtlessly. It wishes only to be your friend (if you are worthy) and not your slave. It retains its free will and will do nothing for that it considers unreasonable.

Thophile Gautier 1811-1872—Human

what someone is saying doesn't mean she's saying the same thing over and over.

One of the definitions of language in *Webster's New World Dictionary* is "any way of communicating," so we can assume that people do have a language and most of you are familiar with the words that your human will use in certain situations. I'm hoping we can help humans learn to see that is what we do too. The biggest problem is that with all the wonderful moving parts of our body that are a part of our language, they often miss the subtleties.

People believe that they can talk to and understand any one of any species. Has your mom ever talked to you in that same voice that she talks to the mini human with the smelly pants? "Oootsy Boootsy Baby, how's my little sweetums. Ooogie boogie baby." Yuck! I taught my mom early on not to speak to me that way. I simply walked out of the room whenever she tried it and she finally curbed the gibberish.

One of the things that is common in many languages is tone. If my mom says "Where did that roll of stamps go?" and her voice is low, I know I better find them and get them back to her quickly. Just as when she is petting my butt and I don't want my butt petted I give her a low "Mmmmrrrrrr" and she will take her hand away.

Another common trait is volume. Mom doesn't yell very much so I know when she raises her voice it is because she

The Cat Box

Cats are a mysterious kind of folk—there is more passing in their minds than we are aware of.

Sir Walter Scott 1771-1832—Human

The Way of the Cat

The Cat Box

The fog comes on little cat feet.

Carl Sandberg 1878-1967—Human

is afraid. This happens sometimes when I start to jump in the oven after she has sprayed some stuff in there. She lets out a very loud "NO!" and I dash under the bed in the other room. She follows me there with a wet rag and washes my paws and fur. It's not really soaking and I think she must be doing it for a good reason because otherwise she wouldn't come near me with water.

I am often made very aware of how little they know of our language when I ask my mom where one of my toys is and she gives me some treats and says "Here you are sweetie, is this what you wanted?"
I don't want to hurt her feelings so I eat the treats and then start asking for my toy again.

On the other hand, when my mom calls my name I perk up my ears and listen carefully and

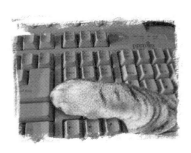

then I go back to sleep. Not because I don't understand her, but because I'm sleeping and I have priorities.

Humans have done research studies to see how we communicate with each other. It seems to me that the only thing they have learned is that although they may not understand what we are saying they do know we are speaking to them. But, how often have you stood in the hallway shouting to your mom and heard only the murmurs of dust bunnies in return? Why? Is your mom ignoring you? Is she hard of hearing? No. She simply doesn't understand the language. She probably thinks you're just telling her that you're home; you're

The Cat Box

If animals could speak, the dog would be a blundering outspoken fellow, but the cat would have the rare grace of never saying a word too much.

Philip Gilbert Hamerton 1834-1894—Human

The Way of the Cat

The Cat Box

If stretching were wealth, all cats would be wealthy.

African Proverb-Ghana

going to grab a quick bite and then take a nap. She just doesn't get it.

This is an amazing technological age we live in. People have devices to communicate anywhere, anytime. Actually, they have used this technology to such a level that they are overwhelmed by all the communications they receive. Emails they don't want from people they don't know. Phone calls from telemarketers trying to sell them things they don't need and tons of junk mail trying to do the same thing. I think that is why they are not honing their communication skills with us. They just don't have the time or the energy it takes to learn our calming, peaceful lan-

The Cat Box

*It is with the approach of winter that cats...
wear their richest fur and assume an air of
sumptuous and delightful opulence.*

Pierre Loti 1850-1923—Human

guage. That is why it is so important that we continue to
try and teach them even when it seems hopeless.

Do humans think we think?

The thing about communication is that *both* parties must
be able to reason—to be able to think. People think we
think on a less complex level than they think. (All right, cut
the giggling.) They think we don't do cognitive thinking.
They think our actions are the result of chance and repeti-
tion. I see no reason to try and change their thinking on
thinking. We are probably better off letting them believe
that they are the superior intellect and that it was just an
accident that the messages
got erased off the answering machine.

There are some humans
who believe we know what
they are feeling, or even
what they are thinking. Of

Cat lovers
are called
Ailurophiles.

The Way of the Cat

course we do and often we even know what they are *going* to think. I know that when my mom finds me sleeping in her office chair in front of her computer she will think about finding something else to do until I get up. I know if she has a lot of work to do she will try to bribe me with treats.

Some humans (very confused humans) think they can train us. Don't be shocked, they do this to dogs all the time, not understanding that dogs are without direction. Dogs need and want to be trained, whereas we are individualists who respond to training in about the same way we respond to water. Sometimes, though, it is the "path of least resistance" to behave in a manner that lets your human believe you are learning what they are trying to teach you. But don't let them overdo it. DON'T DO TRICKS!

Humans are very self-involved creatures. They

The Cat Box

We cannot without becoming cats, perfectly understand the cat mind.

St. George Jackson
Mivart 1827-1900
—Human

---

assume that every other being exists to serve them. Since that is a position we already hold, you can see that communication between us is inherently problematic. But there are ways to get them to understand things without them even knowing that they are being taught. Put some time into understanding them. Watch the way they live, how they take care of themselves, how they eat and especially how they sleep.

- Play with them.
- Cuddle with them.
- Watch what makes them laugh.
- Watch what makes them cry.
- Smell their food.
- Smell their clothing.
- Heck, smell everything.

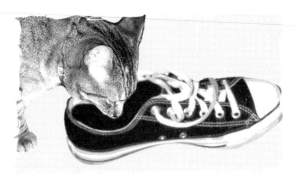

The Way of the Cat

The Cat Box

*A cat's got her own opinion of human beings.
She don't say much, but you can tell enough to
make you anxious not to hear the whole of it.*

Jerome K. Jerome 1859-1927—Human

If you know their general patterns you will know if something has changed. For the good or for the bad. You will know how to react when their moods change and this will only help to keep the home a better space for everyone. Remember, they think of you as part of the family and as part of the family you can be a powerful force for peace and tranquility. These things that come naturally to us are often difficult for people to attain.

What is important is that they at least understand that you are trying to communicate with them. If they have done something to upset you—unroll the toilet paper roll; look for the treasure buried in the plant in the kitchen window; or simply sit and stare at them from some high perch. They don't like that.

Communication is the name of the game

Do you remember the first time your mom rubbed your tummy and you started thumping your tail on the floor to tell her to stop and she still kept rubbing so you turned around, let out a blood curdling scream and wrapped all four of your paws, claws extended, around her arm? Do

---

Dear Xena,
Last week my mom was watching a movie on TV and I kept trying to tell her I'd figured out "Who Done It" but she just kept shhhhuuussshhing me and telling me she wanted to see who the murderer was.

Emily in Edmonton

Dear Emily.
This goes right to the heart of the problem doesn't it. Humans think they are smarter than us. Well if that were true we would be setting our schedule around their lives rather than the other way around. Instead of watching television maybe both you and your mom should be reading a Sneaky Pie Brown mystery.

X

The Way of the Cat

you remember how surprised she looked? She didn't know that thumping your tail on the ground was a very clear message to desist all tummy taps. But she knew after that didn't she? That was communicating.

Your human probably talks her language to you all the time and when she is

> ## The Cat Box
>
> *To err is human—*
> *to purr divine*
> Gracie

up to it she might even try a meow or two. She may try to communicate by touch. She will pet, stroke and rub you, often for her sake as much as yours. She wants to communicate with you. She needs to communicate with you. Help her—in the end you will be helping yourself.

I really like it when my mom strokes the sides of my face. I don't let her do it for too long though. I need to

> ## The Cat Box
> *We know the song they keep in their heart*
> *and purr it back to them when they have*
> *forgotten the words.*
>
> Seth

remain in her eyes detached and distant. So after a brief session of stroking, I walk away. And she never sees the smile on my face.

What body parts are used in communication?

Humans will sometimes use their hands along with their voice to communicate. They have to do this because it seems to be one of the few parts of their bodies they have learned to communicate with. Rarely will you see them position their ears, move their whiskers forward or back, or adjust the size of their eyes. And, of course, they're at a terrible disadvantage due to their lack of a tail. However, I have on rare occasions, seen the hair stand up on the back of Mom's neck.

Finally, what is almost a secret weapon in communicating with humans—the silent meow. Just sit silently

> ## The Cat Box
>
> *With the qualities of cleanliness, discretion, affection, patience, dignity, and courage that cats have, how many of us, I ask you, would be capable of being cats?*
>
> Fernand Mery
> 1897-1984—Human

and look at them. As woefully as possible. Open your mouth a tad, but don't let any sounds out. This old standard is a guaranteed way to get your human's attention and get you some quality petting time. And that is really the bottom line to good communications.

Nuf said.

Legendary Cats

BB

Sara Jane, Bob & Sunny

County

Laurie Lou & Marvin

The Way of the Cat

CHAPTER SIX

A Tail of Two Kitties

"It was the best of times, it was the worst of times..." (My apologies to Master's Cat and Willamina. You'll see why later.)

It would take volumes to thoroughly cover the breadth and depth of our place in history, so this chapter will give you just a few of the highlights.

Although our big cat ancestors have been around for-ever, domestic cats (that's us) have only been around for about four to six thousand years although some cat schools of thought say we have been teaching humans for almost eight thousand years. Maybe it just feels that way. We small cats are descendents of the African Wild Cat. Living in the villages with humans, we ate their food and shared their homes. We were considered an "in-dependent" breed. Yup, it is definitely heredi-tary.

Perhaps the greatest era in our history was our education of the

early Egyptians. They were wise for people; they treated us like gods. We lived in temples eating, mousing and sleeping. We were painted, sculpted and the female humans colored their faces to look like us. (My mom would do well to pay attention to that.) Most importantly, during the Egyptian era it was a crime to kill us, and anyone who did met his own death from a stone-hurling crowd. Just hurting one of our little paws was enough to warrant a human the experience of digital detachment. Bastet, the goddess of love and fertility, was represented as having the head of a cat and the body of a woman. Good choice.

Greek tradition tells how Hacate, a Greek goddess, became a cat to save herself from Typhon, a monster who wanted to have power over heaven and earth. She resumed her original form after Zeus had slain Typhon and we became her favorite animal and she, like us, became symbolically tied with the moon.

Unfortunately, humans have a difficult time sustaining clearheaded thinking and behavior. They tend to go from one extreme to another. And so it

> ## The Cat Box
>
> *Some are born to greatness, some achieve greatness, some have greatness thrust upon them and some are cats.*
>
> Romeo & Juliet,
> companions of William
> Shakespeare

came to be that in the Dark Ages they began killing us and themselves in great numbers because of their un-Egyptian-like religious beliefs, but that did not deter us from coming to their rescue. When the black plague began wiping out entire communities of humans, few were left to continue our destruction so we quickly repopulated. As we grew in numbers we began finding and removing vermin from the human's food supplies. Without the rats, the plague ended. Unfortunately, it was only a matter of time before the humans repopulated and returned to their crusade against us which continued for many, many years.

We came to the United States with the European settlers. Just seeing the Statue of Liberty standing tall in New York Harbor, as our early ancestors did, must have been…oops, that was a little later on.

Most humans are unaware of the deep-seated guilt that they carry from over a thousand years of cat cruelty. They also are unaware that because of this we can make them feel guilty as hell in seconds. Just knowing the amount of control we wield over them is almost always

The Way of the Cat

enough, but every once in awhile it is good thing to reinforce their humility. Bringing a mouse in from outside will remind them, on a cellular level, of those historical events.

Following are just a few standout cats who have been recorded in the annals of history:

Simon, the mascot of HMS Amethyst, was awarded the Dickin Medal in 1949 for "conspicuous gallantry and devotion to duty" during World War II. Many cats served in World War I along the front lines staying with the soldiers in the bunkers and keeping them free of mice.

Calvin lived with Harriet Beecher Stowe, and assisted her in writing her many books.

Scarlett rescued her five kittens by running into a burning building five times to carry them out one by one.

CATS in Moscow. We may have had the longest running show on Broadway, but in Russia 120 of our brothers and sisters play to a 400-member audience. They do a wide variety of tricks and acrobatics to entertain many of Moscow's children.

Patsy lived and flew with Charles Lindbergh.

> # The Cat Box
>
> *Dogs love their humans without restraint—in the same way that humans love us.*
>
> Jackson

Hodge lived with Dr. Samuel Johnson a human who wrote dictionaries and fed Hodge fresh oysters every day.

Orangey starred in television and movies appearing in films like *Breakfast at Tiffany's* and television shows like *Our Miss Brooks*.

Morris is best known to humans for his television role as the 9Lives cat food star, but to most cats Morris is remembered for his support of animal shelters across the country. He himself was found in a shelter in Chicago.

Slippers served in the White House during the Theodore Roosevelt administration.

Tom Kitten served in the White House during the Kennedy administration.

Shan served at the White House during the Ford administration.

Misty Malarky served in the White House during the Carter administration.

Socks served in the White House during the Clinton administration.

Margate served Prime Minister Winston Churchill at No. 10 Downing Street.

Humphrey served at No. 10 Downing Street for eight years.

Andy holds the record for the longest non-lethal fall in our history after falling from the 16th floor of an apartment building.

Beerbohm served for 20 years at the Globe theater occasionally appearing on stage during a play bringing the audience to their feet.

Catarina lived with Edgar Allen Poe and inspired the story "The Black Cat."

Ma lived to be 34 thus holding the record for being the oldest known domestic cat.

Master's Cat was the daughter of **Willamina** and they lived with Charles Dickens. It is to them that I apologize for my humorous usage of text from *A Tale of Two Cities*.

Pulcinella lived with Italian composer Domenico Scarlatti and was known for jumping on Scarlatti's harpsichord and walking up and down the keys. It is said that Scarlatti composed a fugue called "The Cat's Fugue" but my sources tell me Pulcinella wrote it and let Scarlatti have the fame.

Sizi lived with Albert Schweitzer in his clinic in Africa.

Tiger was the companion of English novelist Charlotte Bronte.

Timothy lived with author Dorothy Sayers and wrote two poems with her, "For Timothy" and "War Cat."

Towser lived to be 24 and is credited with having caught almost 29,000 mice. (I don't think my mom would like that very much.)

Trim Trim sailed around the world with his companion Mathew Flinders on the ship Reliance.

Trixie climbed down the chimney that led to the cell of her companion, the third Earl of Southhampton, and stayed with him until he was released two years later.

The list, of course, goes on forever.

Superstitions and myths

* People of many different areas and beliefs would take three hairs from the tail of a cat, put them in a folded piece of paper and then put that paper in a safe place. The next morning when they opened the paper if the hairs were in the shape of an "N" the answer to their question was no, if the hairs were in the shape of a "Y" the answer to their question was yes. I don't know why they didn't just ask the cat.

> # The Cat Box
>
> *The thing that astonished him was that cats should have two holes cut in their coat exactly at the place where their eyes are.*
>
> Georg Christoph Lichtenberg
> 1742-1799—Human

- Sailors have long been superstitious people and attribute many things to us. Some believed that if we meowed loudly when a ship was about to depart it would be a rough trip and if we were playful it would be a good voyage with strong winds into the sails. Some sailors believed that if we licked our fur backwards it would hail and if we sneezed it would rain.
- If we sit or lie with our back to the fireplace it means a cold spell.
- If we tuck our paws under our body it will be foul weather.

MYTH

The Egyptians believed we kept the sun in our eyes at night to keep it safe until morning.

- If we scratch an ear it will rain.
- If we lick our tail it will storm.
- If we wash our face it will rain.
- If they dare to give us a bath it will rain.
  (Judging by those last few superstitions we are quite the meteorologists and we don't even use Doppler radar.)
- In some communities humans would place us in an empty cradle for a newly wed couple to guarantee them children.

- If a black cat walks in their path they will have bad luck.
- If we purr there is a ghost nearby.
- If we sneeze everyone who hears it will have good luck.
- Pulling our tails will bring a human bad luck.
- The Norse believed that we were associated with Freyja who was the mistress of magic. Her chariot was said to be drawn by two of our ancestors who, when they chose, could become horses.
- People believed that our blood and fur could cure ailments.

Dear Xena,

I'm a black cat and I think we have been getting a bad rap from humans. Is there anything that we can do to stop this derogatory profiling?

Pyewackett

Dear Pyewackett;

Pope Gregory the IX declared black cats satanic in the thirteenth century and, of course, during the witch hunts a black cat was always assumed to be a 'familiar' but things have changed considerably over the centuries and humans are beginning to see the greatness in all cats. If I were you though, I would still make an effort to walk across the path of as many humans as possible. They are learning, but they are still superstitious little buggers.

X

The Way of the Cat

- Some believed that the "M" that tabbies still wear on their foreheads first appeared when prophet Mohammed rested his hand on the forehead of one of his beloved cats.

Someday we will have to tell our fables and myths about humans.

"It is a far, far better thing I do…"

Legendary Cats

Marvin

Al E. Cat

Mickey & Pete

Zephyr

Zodiac

The Way of the Cat

CHAPTER SEVEN
Final Thoughts

In the disco era of the '80s we overtook dogs as the most popular house pet. (Stayin' alive, stayin' alive, ooh, ooh, ooh, ooh, ooh.) I know, it's difficult to understand what took so long, but as we have seen over and over again in this book, people can be a little slower than we would like. In the '80s more than 35 percent of American homes housed over 60 million of us and that number keeps growing.

Apparently, humans have finally realized that a barking dog is nowhere near as comforting as a purring cat. Dogs do have their place of course, but even they recognize where—in our shadows. Nothing soothes a human as much as our sitting in her lap and allowing her to pet us.

Human scientists are also beginning to acknowledge the positive effects we have on people. Reports indicate that when we let them stroke us their blood pressure is lowered. A whole lot better than prescription drugs, that's for sure, and you don't even have to go to Canada for a good deal.

> *The stuff called catgut that was once used to make strings for sports racquets and musical instruments **does not** come from cats.*

We are now also recognized for helping senior humans in maintaining mental function; for being excellent companions and generally making them feel better. Some humans have realized that they are going to the doctor less

Dear Xena,

My human has always been a pretty good student, responsive and attentive to my needs, but lately she has been forgetting to feed me, sitting around and staring a lot and basically not much fun. Also there has been another human coming over a lot.

Lucy in Loveland

Dear Lucy;
I hate to tell you this Lucy, but I think your human is in love. It happens to them sometimes and they get really weird. The thing you want to try first is to get this visiting human mad enough to say something mean to you. Your mom will probably throw the other human out. If this doesn't work don't worry. Once the newness is over she will much prefer your company again.

X

and needing fewer medications. They also noticed that what we may consume in cat food, treats and toys is less expensive than doctors and drugs.

People do make an effort to understand us—to do things they think will help us. There are humans that are cat psychics. And some of them help humans communicate with their cats after they have died. (The cats that is.) There are humans who are cat whisperers. They help cats who seem to have personality problems. I know, I know, it does sound strange, but I'm just telling you about them, not making any kind of judgements. Humans may feel that they don't have much to offer us, so they try anything they can.

Most people know what an honor it is to live with a cat and they are aware of how much they need our guidance and emotional support. The list of ways we improve their lives is huge, but I have noted a few below:

- Letting them talk without interruption (as long as they are petting us).
- Making the whole house a playground and every object in it a toy.

- Helping them get up in the morning.
- Helping them stay up in the morning.
- Adding years to their lives.
- Protecting them from mice. Or bringing them mice as gifts, depending on the mood we are in.
- Keeping them smiling.
- Teaching them that no matter how dumb the mistake, you must always act like you did it on purpose.
- POD (Purring On Demand).
- Teaching them kitty yoga (stretching).
- Teaching them the importance of napping.
- Teaching them the importance of napping.
- Teaching them the importance of napping.
- Teaching them the importance of napping.
- Teaching them the importance of napping.
- Teaching them the importance of napping. (Oops, sorry, I got a little carried away.)
- Loving them no matter what they look like, how they dress, what their political affiliations, where they go on

> ## The Cat Box
>
> *The greatness of a nation and its moral progress can be judged by the way its animals are treated.*
>
> Gandhi 1869-1948—A Very Special Human

Sunday mornings, how much money they have (as long as it buys the food), or anything else that humans often use to judge each other.

Does that not describe the ideal companion? Most certainly and that's spelled c-a-t.

Human sayings about cats

I have often wondered where some of these strange cat-related sayings come from. The results of my research may surprise you. Or not.

"Raining cats and dogs"

One theory I have heard about this saying is that back in the days when houses had straw roofs, the cats and dogs (and even the goats) in the area would climb up on the roof to lie on the soft warm material, or we would go up to find the mice that hid there. If it began to rain very hard the animals would be washed off

The Cat Box

A cat has four legs, two ears and a face.
A cat has two eyes that can stare into space.
A cat has great whiskers and feet laced with claws.
But a cat has no boundaries and a cat has no laws.

Author Unknown—
Probably Human

of the roof, thus a hard rain came to be "raining cats and dogs."

Do you want to know what I think? Of course you do. I think somewhere along the way people misspelled the statement. It probably originally read "Reigning cats and dogs."

"Cats have nine lives"

Some humans believe that this has something to do with lucky numbers. Some think it just indicates how well we do under pressure. I think it was an advertising ploy by a cat food company.

"Letting the cat out of the bag"

This one is a little unsettling, but I'll pass along the information I got. It seems that back in the Middle Ages when there were open markets, humans selling pigs would try to cheat another human by putting a cat into a bag and saying that it was a pig. If the buyer

Final Thoughts

were to question the seller's ethics and look into the bag they would see the substituted cat, and therefore "the cat was out of the bag." Is it me, or would you have to be one mighty bad shopper to not look into the bag to see what you were getting?

"Before the cat can lick her ear"

This is one of my least favorite sayings, emphasizing as it does one of our very few limitations. The human author of this little ditty apparently meant that something simply couldn't happen.

That's it then

And now we have come full circle. Back to what we talked about in the first chapter. The best thing you can do for your human is to be a good example. If the bird flies out of your paw before you get a good grip, immediately grab the leaf lying there on the ground next to it and let your human know it was the leaf you were after all along.

Thou art the Great Cat, the avenger of the Gods, and the judge of words, and the president of the sovereign chiefs and the governor of the holy Circle; thou art indeed ...the Great Cat.
Inscription on the Royal Tombs at Thebes

Much of what you have read in this book I'm sure you already knew, but a little refresher course every now and then can't hurt. And the more we know about ourselves, the better we will be able to teach our humans.

The most important thing to remember is that you belong to an elite species and with that membership comes responsibility. To yourselves, to your species and to your humans. For over five thousand years we have been a light in an often dark world. As long as there are cats there is hope for humankind.

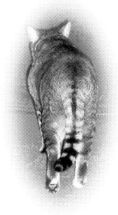

Legendary Cats

Shelby

Cosmo

Jessie

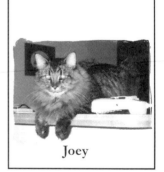

Joey

ZZ

The Way of the Cat

*The ideal of calm exists
in a sitting cat.*
Jules Renard 1864-1910—Human

Order another copy or two

While the memories of all the imformation, humor and awfully cute kitties are still fresh in your mind, it might be a good time to order copies of the book for everyone you know, and their humans too. Just fill out the form below, put it and a check in an envelope and mail it to:

Wellworth Publishing
8400 Menaul Blvd A-136
Albuquerque, NM 87112

Or go to our website at: www..wellworthpublishing.com and order from there. You and all your friends will be glad you did. Thanks, Xena

(Shipping is $3.00 for the first book, plus $1.00 for each additional book shipped USPS Media mail.)

Number of Books ———————

x $14.95 ———————

Plus Shipping ———————

Total ———————

Name _____

Address _____

City _____ St. ___ Zip _____

If you have any questions, please email
jsheldon@wellworthpublishing.com .